Graphic conception:
Sandra Brys

translation: Mollie Dougherty of the
Alliance Française of Boston and Cambridge

© Casterman, Tournai 1994
Published by
Charlesbridge Publishing
85 Main Street, Watertown, MA 02172
(617) 926-0329

Library of Congress Cataloging-in-Publication Data
Duprez, Martine.
    [Animaux qui se camouflent.   English]
    Animals in disguise / by Martine Duprez;
illustrations by Hélène Appell-Mertiny.
       p.   cm.
    ISBN 0-88106-693-1 (library reinforced)
    ISBN 0-88106-673-7 (trade hardcover)
    1. Camouflage (Biology)—Juvenile literature.
2. Mimicry (Biology)—Juvenile literature.
3. Animals—Juvenile literature.   4. Wildlife
conservation—Juvenile literature.   [1. Animals.
2. Camouflage (Biology).   3. Animal defenses.]
I. Appell-Mertiny, Hélène, ill. II. Title.
QL767.D8613   1994
591 . 57 '2—dc20   93-20967
                           CIP
                           AC

ANIMALS IN DISGUISE

by Martine Duprez

illustrated by Hélène Appell-Mertiny

Charlesbridge

"To live long, live hidden!" Many species of animals live by this motto. To survive, these animals use an amazing variety of disguises. For some, the best defense is holding completely still, since their predators have eyes that are especially good at seeing movement. Other animals are masters at blending in with their background. They can change their colors, too. Some predators have learned to disguise themselves to make it easier for them to sneak up on their prey.

Neither seen, nor known

The art of becoming invisible, by changing color and using shapes that match the environment, is called "mimicry." The first scientists to observe animal mimicry were Bates in 1862 and Miller in 1879.

Some animals do not change color rapidly, but instead the species has developed over a long period to match the colors of its natural surroundings. For example, many insects who live on leaves have a greenish coloring. Creatures who live on the ground tend to be brown. In polar areas where the ground is covered with snow, many creatures are white. Spots and stripes help many other animals to blend in with the shadows of tall grasses or leaves.

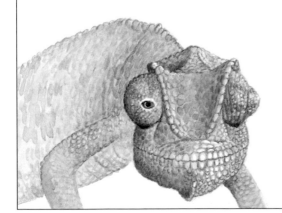

THE DIFFERENT WAYS ANIMALS CAMOUFLAGE THEMSELVES

Color can also be temporary. An animal may take on the color of its surroundings for a moment or a season. The ermine's fur is brown in the summer, but becomes white when winter snow arrives. Some animals can change color quickly. This is the case with the green tree frog, which in spite of its name, can vary its color from brown to yellow. Another example is the flounder which in several minutes can imitate the sandy or rocky bottom of the sea where it swims. The classic chameleon can change color so rapidly that we have come to use its name as a synonym for changeable.

There are also cases when an animal has a shape that helps it hide. The walkingstick, for example, looks like a twig until it moves. Some insects look like a leaf. A frightened hedgehog will roll itself into a ball that looks like the husk of a chestnut.

In another type of mimicry, an animal mimics a different species. Certain harmless species have copied the looks of other, more dangerous ones. The harmless bee fly imitates the yellow and brown stripes of a bee. Birds are afraid of being stung so they leave it alone. By looking like a creature that tastes bad, has a sting, or is poisonous, these copycats avoid being eaten.

Mimicry of form or color is not the only method that animals have for tricking their enemies. Scientists are discovering other forms of mimicry that use smell and light. Certain orchids attract male insects by giving off an odor that smells exactly like a female insect. The art of disguise has created some amazing adaptations in nature.

THE ERMINE

The ermine always seems to be in a hurry. It stands on its hind paws, searching the horizon. Then, quick as lightning, it crosses the road and leaps towards the high grass. It slips through rocks and vegetation, quick as a wink, first into a thick bramble bush, then into the hollow of a dead tree.

To catch its prey, the ermine uses amazing skills. It sneaks up silently on a vole. Then, it jumps on top of its prey unexpectedly, seizes it by the nape of its neck, and kills it with one bite.

The ermine's fur is white during the wintertime. Only the tip of its tail remains black throughout the year. This black tip helps it escape from birds of prey. A hunting bird sees a black spot on the snow. The bird dives towards the spot, but the ermine darts forward and the bird's claws come up empty. Missed by a hair!

8

LOCATION	DESCRIPTION	ENVIRONMENT	BEHAVIOR

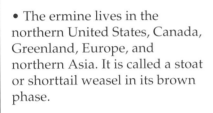

• The ermine lives in the northern United States, Canada, Greenland, Europe, and northern Asia. It is called a stoat or shorttail weasel in its brown phase.

• In summertime, the coat of the ermine is brown on the back and whitish on the stomach. In the winter, its coat becomes white. This is especially true of ermine found in areas where the climate is harsh. Its tail ends with a brush of black in every season.
• The male has a total length of 11 to 18 inches. The tail makes up 2 to 5 inches of that length. The female is 10 1/2 to 14 inches long, with the tail making up to 3 inches of its length.
• The male ermine weighs 4 1/2 to 16 ounces. The female weighs 4 1/2 to 10 ounces.
• The ermine belongs to the mustelidae family which includes the longtail weasel, the badger, the fisher, the ferret, the mink, the skunk, and the marten.

• The ermine lives in fields, hedges, river banks, woods, and thick bush. It also uses hollows under tree roots, low stone walls, and rock caves for shelter. It builds a nest of grass, moss, and leaves, and even uses the skin and feathers of its prey.

• The ermine tends to be nocturnal (active at night) in winter and diurnal (active in the day) in summer.

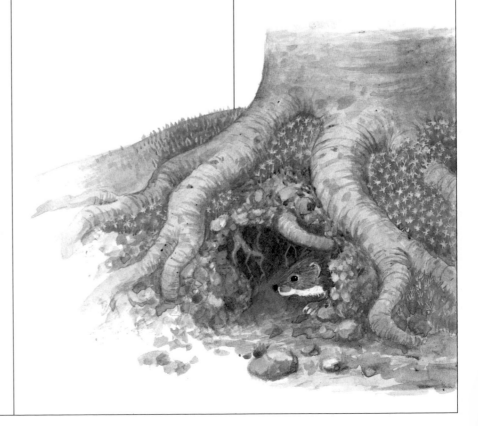

CAMOUFLAGE	REPRODUCTION	FOOD	RISKS, THREATS, AND MEASURES OF CONSERVATION

• In springtime and in autumn, the ermine changes color. A brown coat makes it easier to hide in fields and woods during long summer days. The white winter coat makes the animal nearly invisible when it is hunting on snow-covered winter nights.

• The ermine has only one litter per year. Four to eight babies are born between April and May.

• The ermine eats voles, rats, mice and sometimes moles, shrews, eggs, birds, and fish.
• The ermine will attack prey larger than itself such as a rabbit.

• The ermine is trapped and hunted for its beautiful fur. It is also accused of raiding farmyards and competing with hunters for game.
• The loss of its habitat is a problem in some areas where hedges, dead trees, hollow trunks, and thick bushes are removed.
• In some areas, measures to protect ermine include setting up artificial shelters and bans on hunting it.

THE LEOPARD

The African night fades. As the golden savannah day dawns, sunlight scatters through the clumps of trees. The roars of the lions and hyenas stop. The herds of antelope begin to eat leaves. Its spotted coat blending in with the yellow grass, the leopard inches toward its victim.

One careless antelope is too far away from the herd. Silently, the leopard sneaks toward it, moving from one bush to another, standing still each time the antelope looks around. The antelope lifts its head. It smells danger. It searches the vegetation and sniffs the air. It sees nothing to alarm it. The savannah is so calm that, little by little, the antelope feels safe again and goes back to its meal.

Now the leopard leaps noiselessly from the bushes and lands next to its victim. The antelope tries to escape, but the leopard seizes it by the throat and blocks its windpipe, quietly suffocating its prey.

The leopard drags the antelope up onto the branch of a tree where it eats. After its meal, the leopard rests casually in the shade of the tree.

Little by little, a noise grows on the trail. A car full of tourists approaches and stops not far from the big cat. The guide points to the tree. With binoculars and zoom lenses, the tourists finally see the leopard crouched on the tangle of branches. They cannot believe that this big, beautiful animal could be a fearsome hunter.

LOCATION	DESCRIPTION	ENVIRONMENT	BEHAVIOR

• The leopard lives in all areas of Africa except in the Sahara region. The snow leopard, which is slightly smaller, lives in the rocky mountains of Central Asia. The clouded leopard lives in southeastern Asia.

• The leopard has a very light, tawny colored coat, sprinkled with dark brown groups of spots called rosettes. Its tail is long. Its small, round ears are bordered by a dark black edge. Its claws are retractable (can be pulled in).
• The leopard stands about 3 feet tall at the shoulder. Its average weight is about 125 pounds.
• A carnivore, the leopard is part of the cat family, which includes the tiger, the lion, and the cheetah as well as the house cat.

• The leopard may live in a prickly thicket, along a wooded river, or in a grove of trees. It lives anywhere with water and sufficient prey. It climbs trees to rest or watch for prey and prefers to eat in a tree where other animals won't bother it.

• The leopard is solitary except during the mating season. After mating, in the beginning of the rainy season, the male leopard stays with the female until the babies are one month old. Leopards usually rest during the day and hunt at night.

CAMOUFLAGE	REPRODUCTION	FOOD	RISKS, THREATS, AND MEASURES OF CONSERVATION

• The leopard's spotted coat gives it a natural camouflage with the vegetation of the underbrush.

• The female leopard gives birth to 1 to 6 kittens 95 to 105 days after mating.

• The leopard eats antelope such as impala and gazelle as well as baboons, monkeys, birds, snakes, and fish.
• It drags large prey animals up into a tree where its food will be safe from jackals and hyenas that might try to steal it.

• The leopard is threatened in two ways: it is killed for its fur, and its habitat is being destroyed.
• Today, the leopard is protected by an international treaty that bans leopard hunting and the international trade of leopard skins.
• Leopards are still victims of poaching.

In the moonlight, the shadows of the oak trees stand out clearly. A bat flaps around hunting for insects. The peaceful night is undisturbed except by the sound of frogs croaking in the distance.

Suddenly, humming and scratching noises come from a bush. The grass parts, and a hedgehog appears. Stocky and armed with sharp spines, it moves with small quick steps, nose to the ground. Every once in a while, it stops and sniffs the humid ground, then continues on the trail of its prey. A strange noise makes it tremble. The hedgehog stops completely, ready to roll itself into a ball, offering only a pin cushion to any attacker.

THE HEDGEHOG

A predator who sees this hedgehog will decide to look elsewhere for food. All is quiet. Reassured, the hedgehog begins its walk again. It rounds the hedge, looking for insects, eggs, larvae, or slugs. Instead, it finds a sleeping frog. Yum, yum!

Its meal over, the hedgehog wanders along the edge of a road. Carefully, it steps onto the smooth, hot surface. It knows that here it will find lots of insects to eat. Suddenly, there's a deafening rumbling and a blinding light. Panicked, the hedgehog rolls itself into a ball, with its snout and paws protected under its coat of needles.

The car passes by at full speed. Soon there is nothing left but the noise of a motor that grows fainter in the distance. The hedgehog slowly unrolls itself. It was a close call this time.

LOCATION	DESCRIPTION	ENVIRONMENT	BEHAVIOR

LOCATION

• The common hedgehog lives in Africa, Asia, and Western Europe. Its cousin, the desert hedgehog, lives in deserts and on the Asian steppes.
• There are no hedgehogs in North and South America. The porcupine is quite a different animal.

DESCRIPTION

• The hedgehog has a squat body, a pointed snout, and small, round ears. Its tail is barely visible.
• Its body is covered by coarse hair, and on its back are prickly spines. The spines are white with a brown stripe around the middle and at the top. Its stomach is covered by soft, light brown fur.
• Its body is $5 \frac{1}{2}$ to 12 inches long, of which 1 to 2 inches is the tail. Its height is between $4 \frac{1}{2}$ to 6 inches. It weighs about 3 pounds.

ENVIRONMENT

• The common hedgehog lives in leafy forests, fields, hedges, parks, and gardens.
• Each hedgehog has its own territory varying from 10 to 100 acres.

BEHAVIOR

• The hedgehog is especially active at dusk and during the night. In the day, it seeks shelter in a big nest of grass, leaves, and moss or in thickets bordering fields.
• The hedgehog hibernates from October to April.
• Like many insect-eating mammals, a hedgehog has poor eyesight but a keen sense of smell and hearing which help it know when to roll up into a spiny ball.

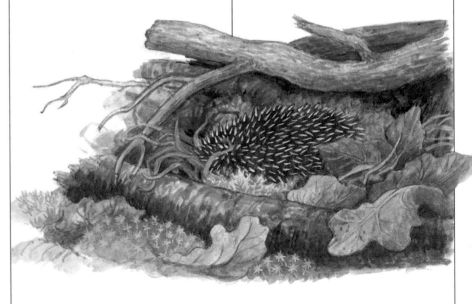

CAMOUFLAGE	REPRODUCTION	FOOD	RISKS, THREATS, AND MEASURES OF CONSERVATION

• The hedgehog is grayish brown in color, but since it goes out only at night and makes a lot of noise when moving, color is not its best disguise.

• At the first sign of danger, the hedgehog rolls itself into a ball. It is protected by its sharp spines which convince predators that it is not edible.

• The female hedgehog has one or two litters a year of 2 to 10 babies. They are born 31 to 40 days after mating.

• The hedgehog eats mainly insects, earthworms, snails, or slugs. Depending on the season, it also eats small frogs, eggs, berries, and fruits.

• At one time, the hedgehog was particularly disliked, and it was the subject of many superstitious stories. Today, people no longer dislike the hedgehog, but people are still its worst enemy. Thousands of hedgehogs are run over by cars each year.

• The hedgehog also suffers from the use of weed killers and pesticides. These products reduce the number of invertebrates that it can find to eat.

• Several protective measures can be taken such as reducing and restricting the use of insecticides and weed killers and protecting the hedgehog's habitat by maintaining and developing hedges, groves, and sources of water.

THE CHAMELEON

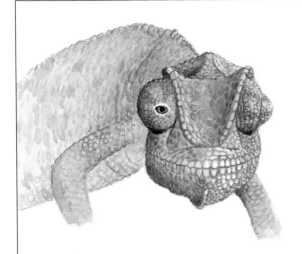

The chirring sound of cicadas resonates through the forest. The wildlife and the trees seem to melt together in the heat of the sun. Meanwhile, unnoticed on a branch, a drama unfolds. With incredible slowness, a mottled brown chameleon moves toward a moth. Almost invisible on the dry branches, the chameleon inches forward.

The prey is not aware of the danger. It continues to gather nectar. Suddenly, the chameleon shoots out its tongue in a fraction of a second! Missed! The moth is fast, too, and moves further away.

The chameleon is not discouraged by this setback and begins its hunting again, still very slowly.

This time, the chameleon's timing is perfect. The moth is caught by the sticky coating on the end of the chameleon's tongue and disappears into its mouth. Satisfied, the reptile returns to its usual stillness. Its coloration allows it to blend in with any background of greens or browns. Its disguise is not perfect, however. This creature sometimes turns black when it feels anger or fear which ruins its disguise.

LOCATION	DESCRIPTION	ENVIRONMENT	BEHAVIOR
• The chameleon lives in Africa, the Middle East, southern Europe, and parts of Southeast Asia and South America.	• Usually soft green, the bumpy skin of the chameleon can change color quickly to become brown or mottled. • The chameleon's body is about 12 inches long. • The chameleon has two protruding eyes which can move independently of each other. • Its only protection is its thick skin and its long toes and grasping tail that it uses to hold on tight to a tree branch. • The chameleon is a reptile. There are seventy types of chameleons.	 • The chameleon lives in forests, low bushes, and undergrowth. When at rest, it usually perches on a branch.	• The chameleon lives alone and is active in the daytime. It can move extremely slowly. • In the mating season, the chameleon may wander away from its usual territory.

CAMOUFLAGE

• The chameleon is able to change color because of special pigment cells in its skin. The cells grow larger or smaller depending upon physical factors such as temperature and light, or emotional factors such as worry or anger.

REPRODUCTION

• The female chameleon lays 9 to 30 eggs that she buries in the ground. Because the egg laying is very tiring, many females do not survive. The eggs hatch after about 250 days of incubation.

FOOD

• The chameleon feeds mostly on insects. Settled on a branch, it usually waits for prey to pass in its range. As soon as it sees an insect, the chameleon slowly approaches it, flips its tongue toward its victim, then snaps its tongue back into its mouth with its food.

RISKS, THREATS, AND MEASURES OF CONSERVATION

• The number of chameleons is decreasing steadily. The species may be on its way to extinction.
• The chameleon suffers from the destruction of its habitat as forests are cleared to make way for buildings. Elsewhere, the spread of pesticides has eliminated mosquitoes, its principal food source. The chameleon is also sought after as a pet.
• The chameleon is protected by a treaty that regulates international trade of threatened species.

THE GREEN TREE FROG

A fine rain moistens the woods and the fields. The birds sing their bright songs. Warmed by the setting spring sun, day once again gives way to dusk. A persistent background noise disturbs the birds' harmony. Ten green tree frogs croak in chorus. The males are courting the females with their singing. These loud croaks give the only sign of their presence.

Their color perfectly matches the flower stems and leaves they sit on. Suddenly, voices drown out the croaking concert. A group of young people, wearing boots and carrying buckets and flashlights, come walking down the road. They place a strange barrier across the pond. It is a long piece of clear plastic stretched between two wooden poles.

The tree frogs are unable to get by the barrier. It keeps them from jumping onto the road where they might be crushed by cars.

The young naturalists gently gather up the frogs in their buckets and move them safely to the other side of the road. Now the male frogs continue their croaking chorus for the female frogs.

LOCATION	DESCRIPTION	ENVIRONMENT	BEHAVIOR

• The green tree frog is present on all of the continents except for Antarctica. It is most common in Australia and the Americas.

• In spite of its name, the color of the green tree frog may be green, yellow, brown, or even sometimes blue, depending on the temperature and its perch.
• The male tree frog has a brown-grey throat sac.
• Its rear toes are webbed and each toe has a suction disc for gripping.
• The tree frog's body is 1 $^1/_2$ to 2 inches long.

• The green tree frog is found in woods, bushes, and on tall grasses.
• During the reproduction period, the female tree frog lays her eggs in the stagnant waters of ponds.

• The green tree frog is mostly active at night.
• It lives in groups.
• Its song can be heard from a great distance at night, depending on the number of frogs in the chorus.
• The tree frog hibernates in ponds or under rocks from fall until spring.

CAMOUFLAGE	REPRODUCTION	FOOD	RISKS, THREATS, AND MEASURES OF CONSERVATION
• To avoid its enemies, a tree frog's best defense is to hold still. Its color, which perfectly matches its immediate environment, helps it remain unseen.	• The green tree frog lays 800 to 1,000 eggs in one night. Several packets of eggs are deposited on plants near the water's edge. At the end of about two weeks, tadpoles hatch. They will grow legs, lose their tails, and learn to breath with lungs by the end of three months.	• The tree frog eats snails, spiders, bugs, and worms.	• The green tree frog is threatened by the disappearance of its natural environment as marshes dry up naturally or are drained. • Pollution from industrial chemicals, fertilizers, and insecticides are also a major problem. • The green tree frog is a victim of collectors who supply pets for terrariums and specimens for laboratories. • It is accidentally run over in areas that are too close to roads. • Environmental protection agencies are trying to reverse the polluted condition of ponds and wetlands. • Some wildlife associations organize rescue operations to help frogs cross roads safely.

THE WALKINGSTICK

The afternoon is drawing to a close. A light breeze, full of the scent of wildflowers, shakes the big birch tree and refreshes the muggy air.

Jason and his sister Kim decide to take a walk. They run across the fields and up the path towards the woods. Breathless and tired, they both agree to rest before following the path to the top of the hill.

They collapse in the grass next to a bush, and cause a bit of panic among the cicadas who were preparing for their nightly concert.

Lying on his back, Jason has his eyes wide open. He looks at the branches of the trees and the small bush next to him. One of the branches catches his attention. Leaning on his elbows, he gets up, and brings his face closer to the branch..."Yikes!"

Jason's outburst makes Kim jump up. Jason points at a branch of the small bush. The branch seems to be greedily devouring one of the bush's leaves. Relieved, Kim smiles.

"Silly, it's only a walkingstick. Its totally harmless!" Then the two children watch the amazing insect together.

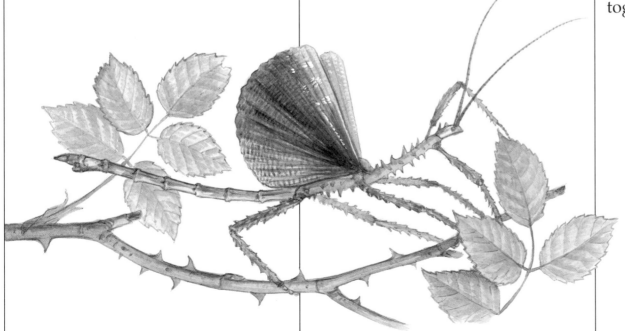

LOCATION	DESCRIPTION	ENVIRONMENT	BEHAVIOR
• There are many species of walkingsticks spread throughout Asia, Africa, and the Americas. They are also found in Europe in the Mediterranean regions.	• Walkingsticks may be green or brown, and resemble leaves and twigs. • Some Asian species are over a foot long, but a more common length is 5 to 6 inches. • Walkingsticks have small heads, a pair of antenna, and three pairs of legs.	• The walkingstick lives in trees and bushes.	• Creatures of the night, walkingsticks generally settle on low plants during the day. At nightfall, they very slowly become active.

CAMOUFLAGE

• The walkingstick looks just like part of a plant. Certain species have the ability to change their color. Some hang by one of their feet and let themselves swing in the wind, like a dead branch.

REPRODUCTION

• The females are much more numerous than the males: 1 male for every 1,000 females. The females can reproduce without having the eggs fertilized by a male! The female deposits eggs on the ground or under loose tree bark. The incubation period is very long, and there are several stages the young walkingsticks must go through before they reach adulthood.

FOOD

• All of the species eat plants, especially leaves and buds. They eat by grinding their food.

RISKS, THREATS, AND MEASURES OF CONSERVATION

• Walkingsticks are not threatened with extinction except in areas where there are fires. It takes a very long time for walkingsticks to re-populate these areas.

Long ago in ancient Rome, Latin authors gave beekeepers who had lost their swarm the following advice, "Place the corpse of an animal in a distant cowshed. Your bees will come and feed there."

How many beekeepers tried this solution? No one can say, but what is certain, is that all who did would have been mistaken.

THE
BEE FLY

The reason the Latin authors gave this advice was that they had observed bee flies. Bee flies, however, do not produce any honey. A bee fly larva feeds on decaying organic matter. Due to its appearance and size, which are identical to that of the bee, this insect has fooled both people and animals. Certain birds avoid swallowing the bee fly because they fear its sting. They do this mistakenly, since the bee fly does not have a stinger and is totally defenseless.

LOCATION	DESCRIPTION	ENVIRONMENT	BEHAVIOR
• The bee fly is very common in Europe and in North America. There are many species of bee flies.	• For the amateur observer, the bee fly and the bee are as alike as two peas in a pod. They are the same size, and both are brown and yellow. That's the end of the similarity. • The bee has four wings; the bee fly has only two. The bee has a curved silhouette; the bee fly has a flatter body.	• The bee fly goes from flower to flower in prairies and fields.	• Typically active during the day, it plays an important role in the pollination of numerous plants, but it does not produce honey.

bee fly

bee

CAMOUFLAGE	REPRODUCTION	FOOD	RISKS, THREATS, AND MEASURES OF CONSERVATION

• Certain birds do not eat the bee fly because its size and color remind them of painful experiences suffered from the true bee's sting.

• After mating, the fly lays its eggs in a muddy pond, a pit of manure, or in a bee's nest. The larvae spend the winter there using a type of siphon to suck up food. Then, they change into flies in a process called metamorphosis.

• Like the bee, the bee fly feeds on pollen and nectar. The larvae feed on decaying organic materials as well as the larvae of the bee.

• The bee fly is abundant and common. As long as manure, garbage, and bees continue to exist, its future is not in danger.

THE FLOUNDER

The flounder we see on our plates may not impress us as unusual, but this fish leads a rather artistic life. Its color changes help it to hide so that it can wait for food to swim by. Many scientists are interested in its skills.

The flounder changes color to match the colors of the bottom of the sea where it lies. Now it is in a bay where the bottom is covered by pebbles and shells, so it is spotted white and brown. As it swims away, under the bridge, into the inner harbor, the bottom becomes dark grey mud. Within a couple of hours, the flounder has become a dark grey to match it! The flounder can match patterns that are spotted or even striped.

The flounder has come to the inner harbor to lay her eggs. She lays thousands of them. Nearby, the eggs from another flounder are hatching. As a baby flounder emerges from its egg, it swims upright like any other fish, and its eyes are on opposite sides of its head. As it grows, it begins to topple over and to swim lying on one side. Then its head twists sideways so that the eye on the downward side is facing up. For the rest of its life, it will swim lying on its side, close to the bottom of the sea.

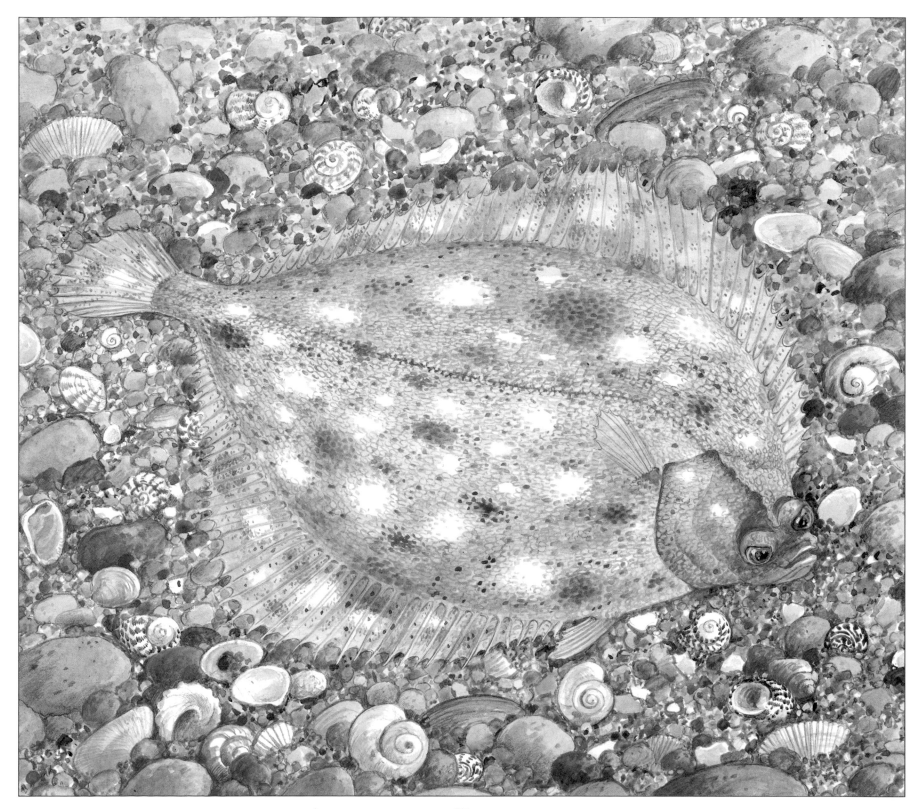

LOCATION	DESCRIPTION	ENVIRONMENT	BEHAVIOR
• The flounder is one of a family of flatfish (teleosts) that can be found in all seas. Other fish of this family are fluke, halibut, turbot, sole, and plaice.	• The flounder is not symmetrical. As an adult, both of its eyes are on one side of its body. The side of its body that faces the bottom of the sea is whitish. Only the side facing up takes on the color of its surroundings. • Most of its teeth are on its downward side. • Flounder used to be almost 3 feet long. Today, because of extensive fishing, they rarely reach that size.	• The flounder lives on the bottom of the sea in sand, mud, or pebbles, near the coast and to a depth of 650 feet.	• The flounder hides when hunting. Thanks to its camouflage, its prey do not see it lying in wait and its enemies do not notice it unless it moves.

CAMOUFLAGE	REPRODUCTION	FOOD	RISKS, THREATS, AND MEASURES OF CONSERVATION
	• Each female can lay up to 500,000 eggs that drift with the currents.		• Flounder suffer from intensive fishing, which reduces the size of its species. They also suffer from pollution when pesticides and industrial chemicals wash down the rivers into the ocean.
• Adult flounder have the ability to change their color because of special pigment cells under their skin. These cells change color by becoming larger or smaller.	• Babies hatch from the eggs after 17 days. Their eyes are on opposite sides of their heads, and they swim along upright as most fish do.	• Flounder feed on a number of invertebrate species (those without backbones) such as snails, marine worms, and shrimp.	• One remedy for these problems is controls on intensive fishing. In some areas, quotas have been established so that only a set number of flounder can be caught. Pollution can be controlled by limiting or even prohibiting the use of pesticides and by controlling the amount of industrial waste discharged into the sea.

THE ALPINE PTARMIGAN

The low and wispy clouds cover the sky, and powdery snow coats the ground in a spotless, white velvet blanket. The snow-capped mountains are wrapped in silence. In this world of complete whiteness, a raucous cry suddenly shatters the silence.

Little by little, in the dizzying whiteness of the countryside, a form slightly larger than a pigeon emerges. The alpine ptarmigan is almost invisible. Its enemies cannot see it, and it is perfectly comfortable in the cold. It has a cave hollowed out in the deep snow that serves as a shelter.

In the spring, the male unfolds his winter feathers to attract females.

The contrast between his plumage and the countryside is striking. He will fiercely defend his territory against potential rivals.

In summer, the countryside changes appearance. This time, the ptarmigan does, too. A ptarmigan loses its white feathers and becomes tawny gray with little, dark brown spots. It is difficult to see the ptarmigan in summer because it is the same color as the mosses, lichens; and heathers of the tundra.

The ptarmigan can hide from its natural enemies, but unfortunately, no feather color will hide it from tourists and hunters.

41

LOCATION	DESCRIPTION	ENVIRONMENT	BEHAVIOR

• The alpine ptarmigan is about 14 inches long.
• Part of the alpine ptarmigan's wing stays white all year round, and some of its tail feathers stay black all year long, but its body has three changes of color: white in winter; tawny gray, spotted with dark brown in spring and in summer; and finely spotted gray in autumn. The male has a bright red comb.
• The alpine ptarmigan is part of the grouse family (tetraonidae) and belongs to the order of galliformes.

• The alpine ptarmigan lives in Arctic regions in mountainous and rocky areas as well as on the tundras.

• The alpine ptarmigan is a solitary and territorial creature. The male fiercely defends its area against all intruders.

• The alpine ptarmigan can be found in Arctic regions of Alaska, the northern United States mountains, Canada, Iceland, North Scotland (1,980 feet above sea level), and in the mountains of the French Alps and the Pyrenees (6,600 feet above sea level).

CAMOUFLAGE	REPRODUCTION	FOOD	RISKS, THREATS, AND MEASURES OF PROTECTION
• The feathers of the alpine ptarmigan adapt to the colors of the seasons. As soon as the first snow falls, the gray feathers that it wears in autumn become white, except for the tail feathers that remain black. In summer, the ptarmigan is tawny gray, spotted with dark brown. It, therefore, blends in perfectly with its surroundings.	• Between May and July, the female ptarmigan lays 6 to 10 lightly spotted eggs. • The incubation lasts for 21 to 24 days.	• The alpine ptarmigan feeds on buds, berries, and wild grains, but it will eat occasional snails, worms, and insects.	• The population of the alpine ptarmigan, which is already small, is declining. • The principal dangers that threaten the alpine ptarmigan are hunting and tourist activities associated with skiing that interfere with its habitat.